Table of Content

MW00453586

The Jam

By: Laura Nicholas

Pat is a cat.

Pat has a pal.
The pal is Max.

Pat and Max had jam.

Pat has the jam cap.

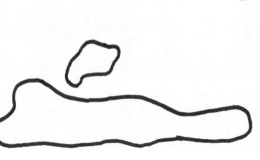

M

Pat is sad.
Max is sad.

Pat and Max dab the jam.

Pat is not sad.
Max is not sad.

The Map

By: Laura Nicholas

Pat and Max sat on a mat.
Pat has a map.

The map has an 'X'.

Pat and Max nab a cab.

Pat ran.

Max ran.

Pat and Max got a pan and ham.

Pat and Max had ham.

Pat can nap.
Max can nap.

The Pig

By: Laura Nicholas

Pat is at a bin.

Pat can get a pig.
It is a big pig.

The pig is on the mat.

Max can get the pig.

Max can tip the pig.

Max can pat the pig.

Max and the pig can dig.

Max, Pat and the pig sit.
Max, Pat and the pig sit on the mat.

Mix

By: Laura Nicholas

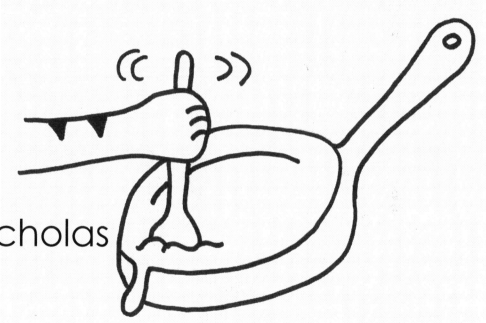

Pat is in the hut.

Pat can get a pan.
Pat can get a bib.

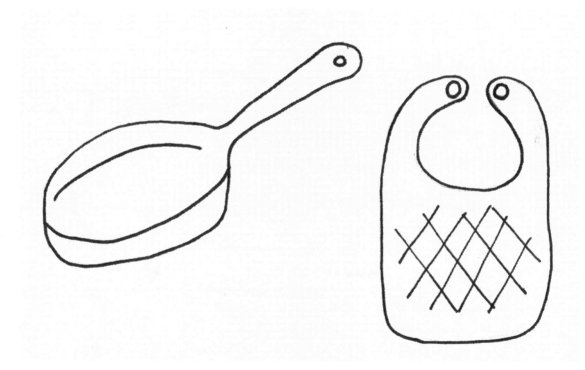

Pat can dip it.
Pat can mix it.

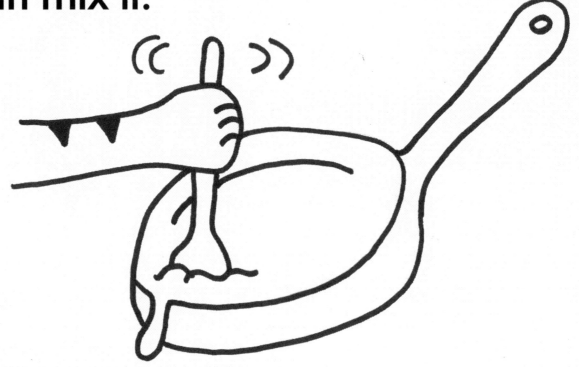

Pat has a bun.
Pat can nip the bun.

Max can nip the bun.
Max has a bit on his lip.

Pat and Max can sit.

The Box

By: Laura Nicholas

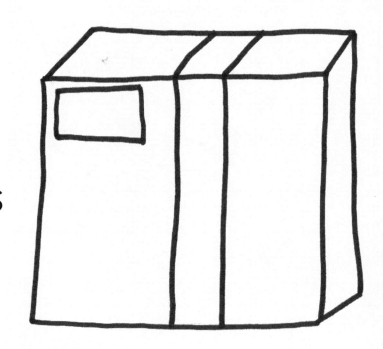

A man is at the hut.
Pat can get a box.

Is it a top?
Is it a pot?
Is it a rod?

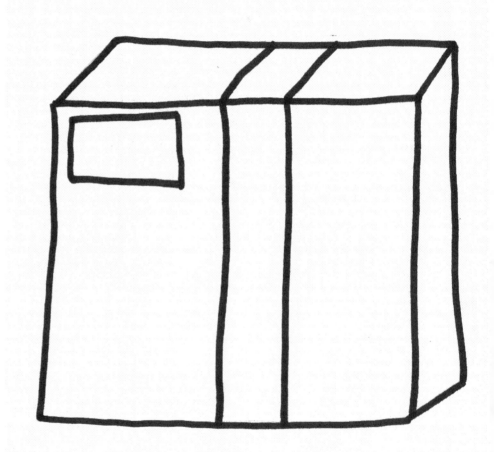

It is six cod!
Pat is not sad.

Max can get a cod.
Max is not sad.

Pat and Max can nap.

The Top

By: Laura Nicholas

Pat has a mom.
Mom is a big cat.

Mom has a top.
Pat can get the top.

The top is on the box.

The top is on the log.

A hog can get the top.
Pat can sob.

Mom can get a top.
Pat is not sad.

The Pet

By: Laura Nicholas

Pat and Max get a pet.
The pet is an egg.

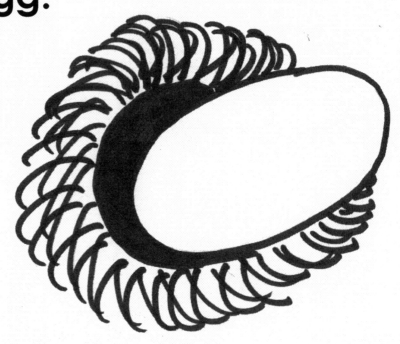

Pat and Max tap the egg.

The hen is not in the egg!

The hen is at the end!
Max did not get it.

Pat can get a net.
The net can get the hen.

Pat can set the hen on the mat.
Pat and Max pat the hen.

The Bed

By: Laura Nicholas

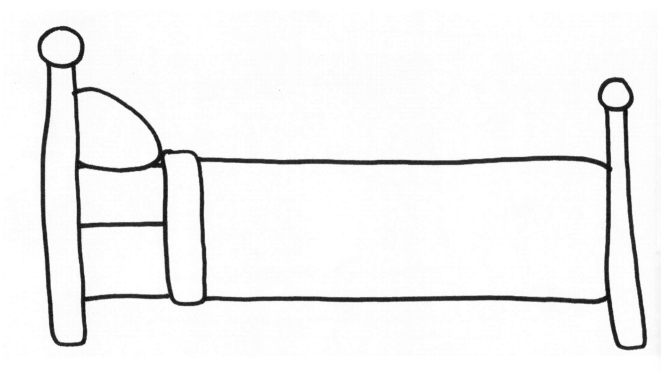

Pat has a bed.
It is a big bed.

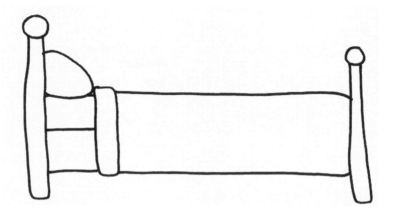

Pat and Max sit on the bed.

Pat and Max hop on the bed.
Pat and Max had fun.

Max hit his leg.
Pat can rub Max on the leg.
Max is not sad.

Pat can nap on the bed.
Max can nap on the bed.

The Bug

By: Laura Nicholas

A web is in the hut.
Pat and Max sit.

A bug is on the web.
The bug is not big.

Pat can get a cup.
The cup is a mug.

Pat can get the mug up.

The bug is in the mug.

The mug is not in the hut.
The bug is not in the hut.

The Sun

By: Laura Nicholas

Pat is hot.
Max is hot.

The sun is hot.

Max can get a fan.

Pat can get a tub.
Pat can get in the tub.

Max can get in the tub.
Max can sit in the tub.
Max is not hot.
Pat is not hot.

The Jet

By: Laura Nicholas

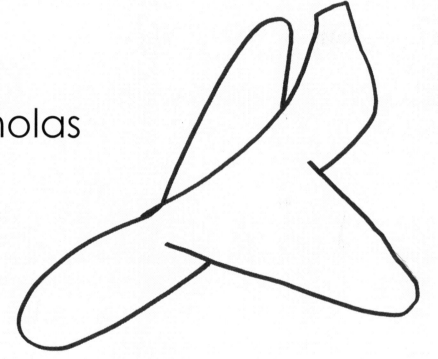

Max has a jet.
The jet is not big.

The jet is up!

The jet is up.
Max is sad.
Max can sob.

Pat can tap the jet.

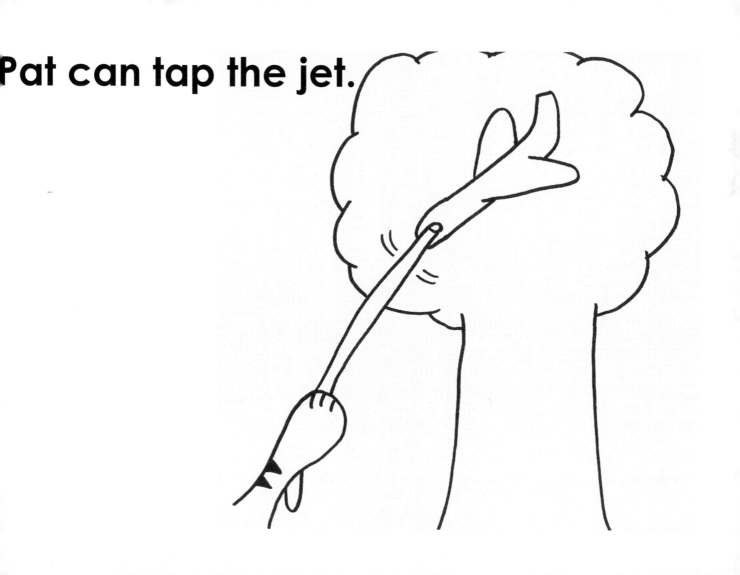

The jet is off.

Max is not sad.
Pat is not sad.

The Bag

By: Laura Nicholas

A bag is on the mat.
Max is at the bag.

Max can tip the bag.
An egg is in the bag!
The egg is on the mat!

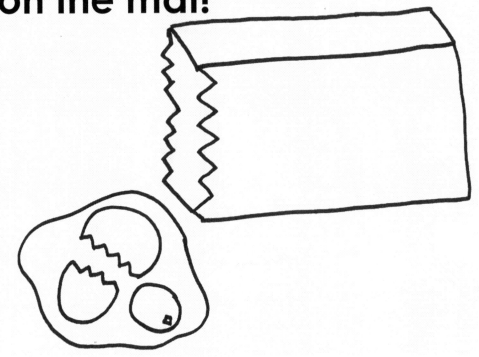

Max is sad.

Pat can mop up the egg.
Max can rub the egg.

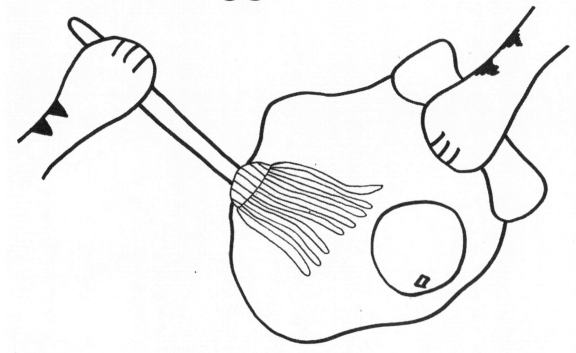

Pat is not sad.
Max is not sad.

MADE-IN
4U6

USA
SH.17

MAde -iN
+he

Made in the USA
San Bernardino, CA
02 November 2019

USA

SAN

59349816R00049